Li'l Lisa

Gemma Gargrave

BookLeaf Publishing

Presentation by *BookLeaf Publishing*

Web: www.bookleafpub.com

E-mail: info@bookleafpub.com

ISBN: 9789357445139

First edition 2021

DEDICATION

For Rudi, Xanthe and Fox:

Whatever it is, just go out and do it. Apart from that, of course. x

ACKNOWLEDGEMENT

With thanks to my family for their relentless love and support; especially my husband, Jack, who consistently indulges my every whim and tirelessly works to drown out the self-doubt. This wouldn't have been possible without you.

Intro

This is a poem all about how
I rhymed some words and wrote them down
Formed some couplets, nice and tight
Rapped them out loud to check they're alright

Well, my kids look disgusted, won't do that again
Don't want them to film it and send to a friend
Again and a friend? Not really a rhyme
But if you say it quick then I'm sure it is fine

Rhyming is hard! And deep down you know it
Otherwise everyone would just become a poet
So ignore the words and just enjoy the rhythm
How the hell am I going to rhyme something with rhythm?
Guess I could try to rhyme it with with'em
But it depends how you say it, it isn't a given

So maybe I won't try to find it a friend
Not all poems have to rhyme, right?

(That's the end.)

An Ode to Monday

Sweet symbolic enemy of the working West
Productive citizens bemoan your grace
As they:
Dredge themselves out of their slumber,
Place the shackles of sadness upon their limbs,
Use their own key to lock themselves up
Whilst summoning the souls of their
professional profiles
From wherever they left them on Friday at 5.

Trading precious life-minutes for an eternity of
servitude,
Acting like Monday is really the problem.

Firsts and Lasts

When your babies stop being babies
They walk
They talk
Use knife and fork
They've started school
Slept right through
Given kisses
Said 'love you'
All major milestones been and gone...
What firsts will we have now?

First time they shout they hate you
First time wishing for a different mum
First time you take their phone away
First weekend banned from PS4
First week banned from PS4
First fortnight banned from PS4
Banned from Fortnite forevermore
Don't they just love to push their luck?
First time saying 'shit' and then comes 'fuck'
First time broken by comments from a friend
First time fighting with you like it just won't end
First time keeping all their feelings in
'Til they eventually pour out
First time showing they still need you

(if you ever had a doubt)

I think about the baby firsts
All pure and good and gone too fast
And now I drink up all of it
While dreading all the lasts.

Li'l Lisa

I want to be like Lurleen Lumpkin,
Talented and flirty
Or maybe just the girl-next-door
like Mindy and her turkey.

I'd love to be Luann,
The bold and brash Van Outen.
Or saucy Malibu Stacey;
plastic curves and perfect pouting.

I'd gladly be Ruth Powers,
Dangerous and exciting.
Or maybe even good old Marge,
all homely and inviting.

Or babysitter Laura,
Whose Hertz Donut won Bart's heart...

But if I'm really honest
I've been a Lisa from the start.

My Nan

Take a Break and teapots
Pinning rollers every night
Pineapple jam on toast for supper
Tucking us up tight

Bungalows, conservatories
Bars of imperial leather
Apple turnovers from the bakery
Long walks in any weather

Carrier bags inside our wellies
For playing in the snow
Standing at the door to wave us off
Each time we go

The blue and white striped pushchair
For Tiny Tears and Golden Ted
Waking up too early
Climbing in Nan's side of the bed

Watching Dinnerladies
Or Jerome in London's Burning
Countless knitting lessons
(But never really learning)

Handmade matching jumpers
The very best roast dinners
When it comes to Nanny lotteries
We really were the winners.

Read More Books

The libraries need saving -
not just temporary reprieves -
the fight continues on to prove
that books are what we need.
Fighting well-read politicians,
who downplay education
because the only thing they're scared of
is an educated nation.

Chicken Quiche

The finest of ingredients
(organic is a must)
Precisely measured, poured with love
Into a tasty, flaky crust.

You're made of all the good stuff
In a sexy, savoury flan
You are eggy
and you're messy
You are proper tasty scran

Some may love you, some may not
But you'll always fill my niche
You are perfectly imperfect
You're my ideal chicken quiche.

Here's Looking at You, Pal

Orange rain and yellow moods
Tear-stained pillows, crumbed with food
Heavy heads host heavy frowns
No more ups, it's always downs
Mop up spills with a piss-soaked towel
Here's Looking at you, pal.

Benjamin Lay

Benjamin Lay was an interesting man
Whose life almost reads like it's fiction
1682 born, 1759 died
77 years lived with conviction

An Essex man, a Quaker,
Who had no fear of rapture
The life and times of which he had
Really dwarf his stature

He travelled well and lived his life
Alongside his wife, Sarah,
Demanding freedom for all slaves
Insisting life be fairer

From England to Barbados
To the states he took his mission
Fighting inequality
And touting abolition

No-sugar vegetarian
For whom greed was a crime
Plain clothing, an impressive beard
A hipster before his time

He'd turn up at the meeting house
With a point to prove
He'd lay out in the freezing snow
And just refuse to move

Fake blood and theatrics
A nuisance with a cause
His commitment to his principles
Laid groundwork for new laws

He frequently was carted off
For causing a commotion
To him it was in servitude
Acts of pure devotion

He made the world a better place
Although his life was tough
Benjamin's an unsung hero
And we can't thank him enough

And thanks to Marcus Rediker
Who literally wrote the book,
Presenting all the details
(I suggest you take a look).

Another Unsung Hero

Giraffes are far superior
To lions and tigers and sharks
Their elegant necks place them above
All gossip and rude remarks

They dish out pure eyelash envy
Their pattern so modern and chic
Long legs giving regal realness
They're charming and cool and unique

Safari supermodels
Aloof and doing their thing
If you ask my favourite animal
Giraffes will always win.

Homework

I never thought I'd be 32
Still crying over homework
Left to the last minute
(Yet a-fucking-gain!)
The panic sets in that's it all wrong
But there's just no time to check.
A little voice says 'I can't do it!'
My brain screams 'please just try!'

I never thought I'd be 32
Still crying over homework
I'm just glad this time the homework isn't mine.

102

Imagine if all the searching for the fountain of youth
The elixir of life
An existence with purpose
Is all just a lie?
A game
A wild goose chase

If Darla Jones from down the road
has it all figured out
She smoked 60 a day
Fitting them in around scrubbing the steps
Eating tinned meat
Walking miles every day
In just her bare feet

Watching family and friends fading away
You're the only one left
Thirty years pass
Thirty years full of days
Cared for by people on minimum wage

Another birthday rolls around
You're wheeled out, again, to that room
With that cake

The papers have come for your secret to age

The answer is still the same as last year
But you can't just say
It's a mix of good genes,
food to eat,
and enough money left to pay for some heat.

And they're not interested in your stories
So you don't share them again.

Come on, Darla, what's your secret?
"Drink red wine and stay away from men."

My Bed

I made my bed
I'll lie in it
Perched atop a mattress stuffed with

Unfinished projects
Forgotten hobbies
Fleeting dreams
Angsty daytimes
Itchy feet
Busy days
Restless nights
Irrational fears
Rational terrors
New obsessions
Old concerns

All sharp corners
Broken springs
Lumps and bumps
And awkward stains

I'll sleep on you for years
But I won't get any rest.

Coco Loco

Scooping shit, muddy paws
Wrestling stuff from needled jaws
Rancid food that smells like tripe
Random barking through the night
Licks her bum then licks your face
Doesn't care about personal space
Steals all the cover, ransacks the bin
Woofs at the postie, will let no one in.

An utter liability, she sends me bloody loco
But I can't imagine life without
My rescue puppy Coco.

A Sani-Tea Ritual

The clear water babbles
In the peaceful bay of Kettle
The bubbles lap against the sides
In the brook of shiny metal

Until it wants your attention
It gives off a chilling scream
You reach for the receptical
That's hidden in the steam

You think you choose a vessel
But in truth it chooses you
A birthday gift, a sentiment
Any old thing won't do

You owe it to yourself
To be fussy
To feel fuzzy

The pyramid in your palm
Hides a hundred secret leaves
Each pyramid contains
At least one answer that you need

Dunk

Dunk
Squeeze
Stir
Dunk
And squeeze again

Add a swirl of light
Just a splash to soften up
Use a dainty spoon
To stir some balance in your cup

The final stir
The final squeeze
Shake the bag
Then sit and breathe

Tiny drops of happiness
Traverse the ridges of your lips
Little kisses on the cup
Send drops of moisture on their trip

Until it reaches the right climate
Not too cool but not too hot
Without any further ceremony
Big gulps finish the lot.

Jeff the Fish

We are gathered here today
To mourn the loss of Jeff the Fish
He was here, until he wasn't
Now he will be sorely missed.

Festival Fling

On the first day, I'm erected.
You manipulate my poles,
Putting the right bits in all the right holes.
I shudder as you bang me into the ground.

You enter me and rummage around,
Depositing your baggage, filling me up,
You laugh with your friends as you fill up your cup.
A drink has been spilt and I'm getting wet.

I eagerly wait for the towel to arrive,
To get me rubbed down to protect my insides.
But it doesn't come.
You don't come.

It's pouring outside and the door starts to drip
Where you've been heavy-handed and damaged my zip.
I'm left open,
The rain penetrating my skin.

Music pounds in the background.
I think of you out there, dripping wet,
But you're not coming home to my warmth

Not yet
I'm alone, trembling in the wind.

The last day rolls around, I'm softer this time,
Standing less proud
Battered and used, just one of a crowd
As your fingers tug my broken zip...

I know.
This is the final time.

I've been used for a weekend,
Left behind in a field.
You won't come for me again.

Secret Admirer

I love you and adore you
In a million little ways
I try to let you know it
As we navigate the days.
All the normal boxes ticked
But it's not them that light the fire
It's the million other little things
I secretly admire.

The way you spend your Fridays
Getting drunk and cleaning up,
The way you bitch and moan
About me using every cup.
The way that you love music
And the way you teach guitar,
The night times watching Family Guy,
Your laughter from afar.

The way you read kids stories
With all the perfect voices,
The way you ban me from cooking
When I struggle making choices.
The way you make my lunches,
The way you always drink my drink.
The way that your face changes

When you really need to think.

Your profile when you're driving,
That pair of big strong arms.
The way you can meet anyone
And hook them with your charms.
The way you love an audiobook
And that fucking Simon Mayo,
The way that just no matter what
You always make my day-o

The way you sing the wrong words,
The ways you drive me mad.
All the ways that you're my husband
And the ways that you're their dad.
The hundreds of ideas
That we never did pursue,
The way you talk with confidence
When you haven't got a clue.

The way you cut my toe nails
And you let me cut your hair,
The way you ask for my opinion
And I know you really care.
The way you always doubt yourself
Even when you're right.
The way you cross your arms
When it's been a heavy night.

The plans to quit the rat race,
Start a cult and just retire...
That's just some of the ten million things
I secretly admire.

Of Sleep and Death

Sleeping beauty
One arm, curved
Lingers on the pillow.
Awake.
Conflict.
Flesh.
Stress.
What quiet friend -
Too easy to forget that you are life itself.
Life and death, together.
Sat at the end of this world,
So childlike, calm
And yet I stoop and I see
Loneliness.
Myself.
Standing within sleep.

Friday

Spring in your step
It's Friday
It can wait til next week
It's Friday
More shirking than working
It's Friday
Sneak out three minutes early
It's Friday
Let your hair down
It's Friday
Pour a big gin
It's Friday
Thank your capitalist overlords for the
impending two days off, honouring your need
for that sacred weekend
It's Friday
Unless you work in hospitality or retail or
entertainment or any other industry where they
don't give a fuck if
It's Friday

Not A Poet

I'm not a poet.
Just a person who sees beauty
Pain
Sadness
Love
And tries to convey them on the page.

But not a writer.
Just someone who jots down
Plans on a napkin
Text on a phone
Furious scribbles on envelopes.

But not an artist.
I just spend my spare moments
Moulding words into form
Crafting a narrative
Sculpting a picture of the things that I'm not.

Okay, maybe I am an artist after all
I could call myself a writer
Declare myself a poet
Since I've made this:
A book.
A book of actual poems.

www.ingramcontent.com/pod-product-compliance
Lightning Source LLC
Chambersburg PA
CBHW051752130826
49812CB00033B/1112
* 9 7 8 9 3 5 7 4 4 5 1 3 9 *